William Bee's Wonderful World of

TRAINS

and Boats and Planes

PAVILION

First published in the United Kingdom in 2017 by
Pavilion Children's Books,
43 Great Ormond Street, London WC1N 3HZ

An imprint of Pavilion Books Limited.

This paperback edition first published in the United Kingdom in 2019.

Publisher and Editor: Neil Dunnicliffe
Art Director: Lee-May Lim
William Bee's Agent: Jodie Hodges

Text and illustrations © William Bee, 2017
Photographs of the Moon and Earth used courtesy of NASA

The moral rights of the author and illustrator have been asserted.

ISBN: 9781843654155

A CIP catalogue record for this book is available
from the British Library.

10 9 8 7 6 5 4 3 2 1

Printed by Toppan Leefung Printing Ltd, China
Reproduction by Tag Publishing, UK

William Bee's Wonderful World of
TRAINS
and Boats and Planes

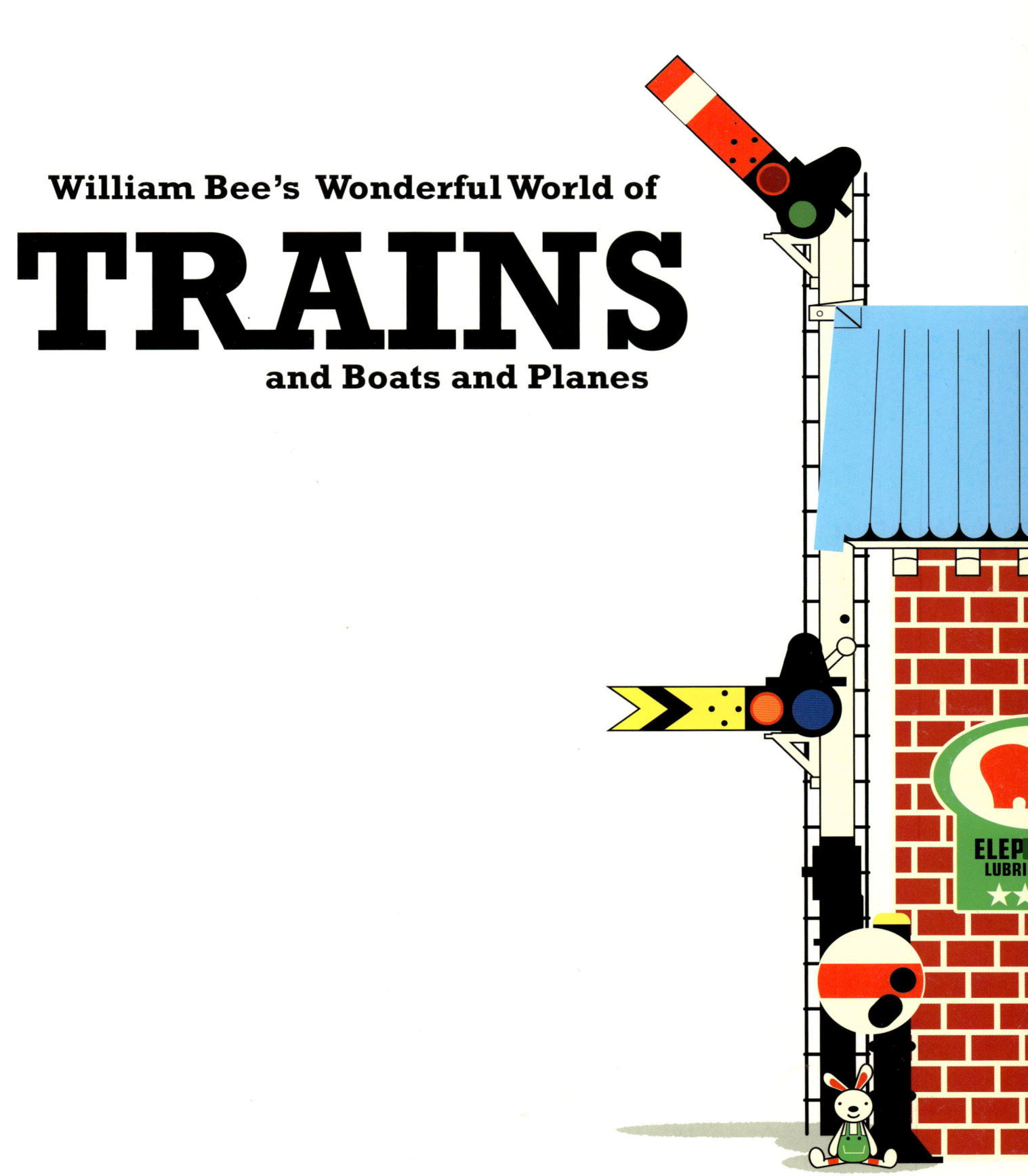

Hello. I am William Bee, and this is my Wonderful
World of Trains and Boats and Planes.

WILLIAM BEE'S ENGINEERING WORKS

LOOK OUT
FOR
TRAINS

STAR
TOOLS

PARTS

GREASE

ELEPHANT
WHITE
GREASE

Once upon a time, the only way for people to get around was by walking, or on the back of a horse, or in some sort of contraption that was pulled by a horse.

And then along came...

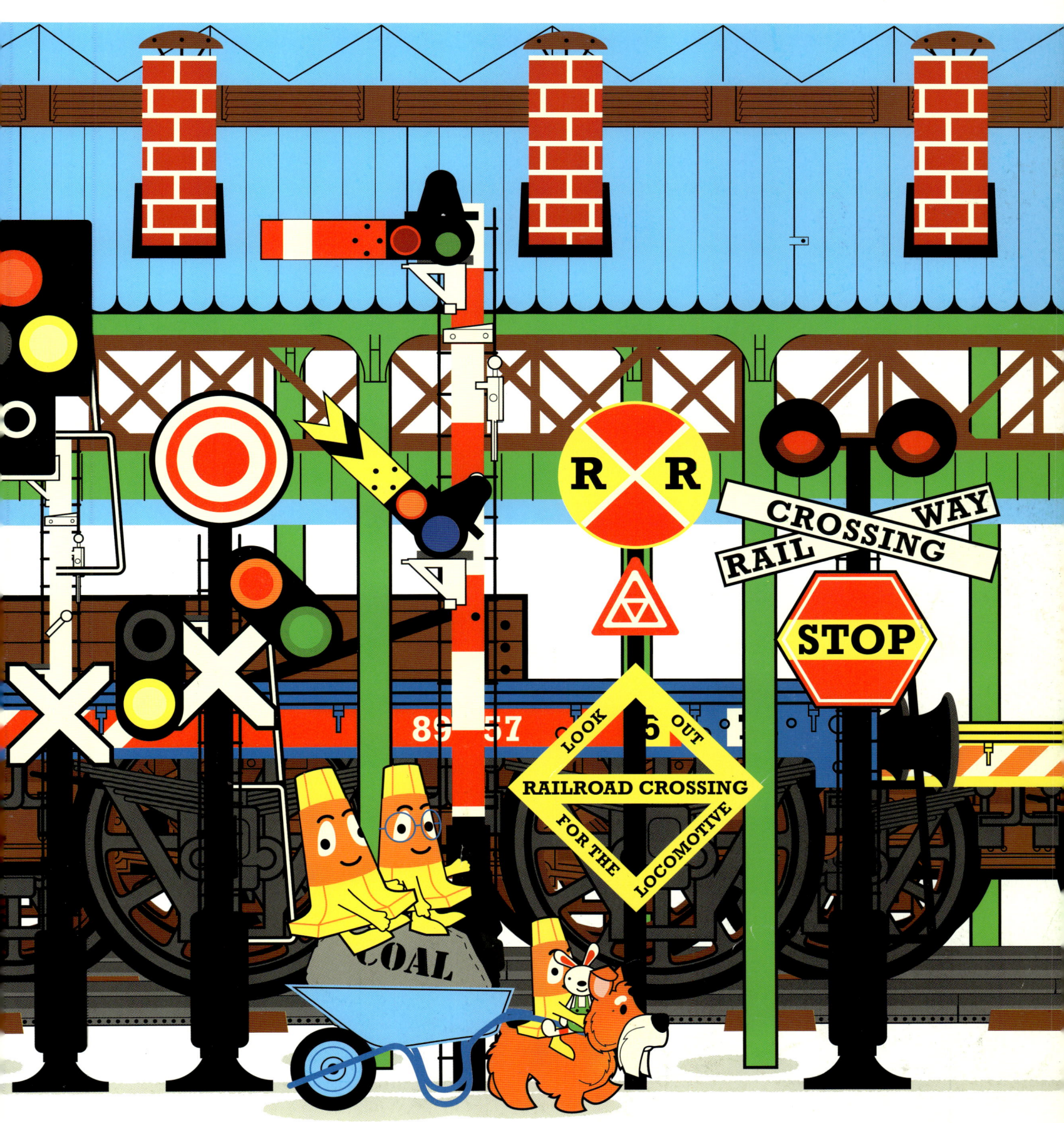

...the steam engine! Which is much faster than a horse –
and much stronger than a horse, too.

The only real problem is that you have to get up REALLY early to stoke the fire and build up the steam to get it going. Four or five hours early.

So that is why I also have...

...a diesel-powered train.

You fill it up with fuel just like a bus or a truck.
And once it is full it is ready to go.

However, it does use ever such a lot of diesel, and you do have to keep filling it up, over and over again. So I also have...

...this high-speed super-sleek non-stop electric train. The electricity comes from a power station, through the overhead cables you can see above the train.

So long as there isn't a power cut, it just keeps on going and going and going.

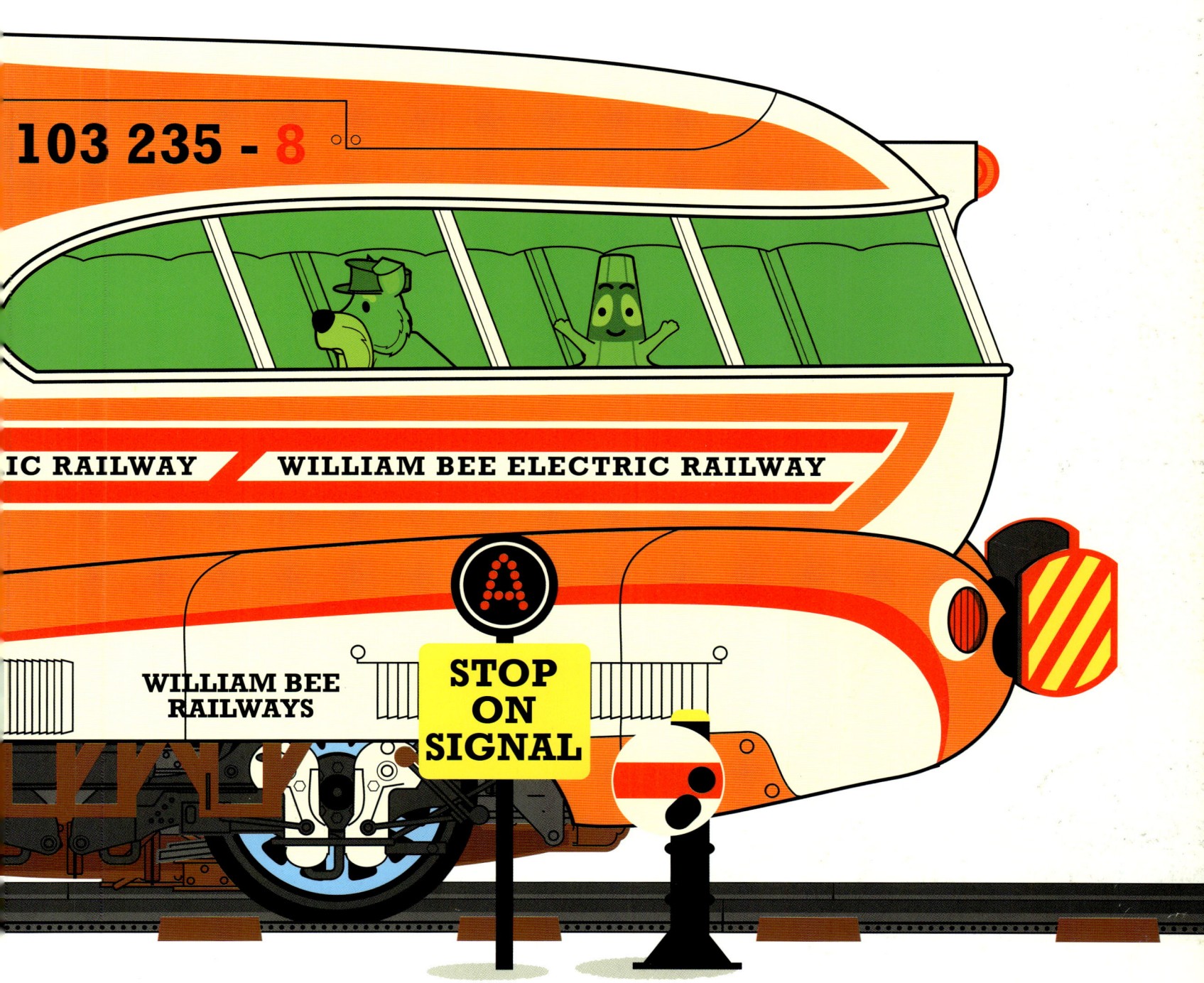

Or it would do if we had laid enough track!

Luckily I have something that does not need track (or a road), because it can hover.

My hovercraft has giant fans which push air underneath it and raise it up off the ground, or the sea, or a swamp, or pretty much anything. The engine then pushes it forward.

Hovercrafts are very impressive, but not as impressive as what lives in this little wood.

It's a vertical-take-off jump jet. It can go straight up in the air, and straight down. It can turn around and around and when it is facing in the direction it wants to go, it can go at 730 miles per hour.

When it comes home it can hide in the little wood, and no-one knows it is there.

That plane was made of technology and gizmos and all sorts of scientific inventions, but this one isn't. It's made from canvas, wood and glue.

You have to fly it very carefully, or...

...it goes upside down!

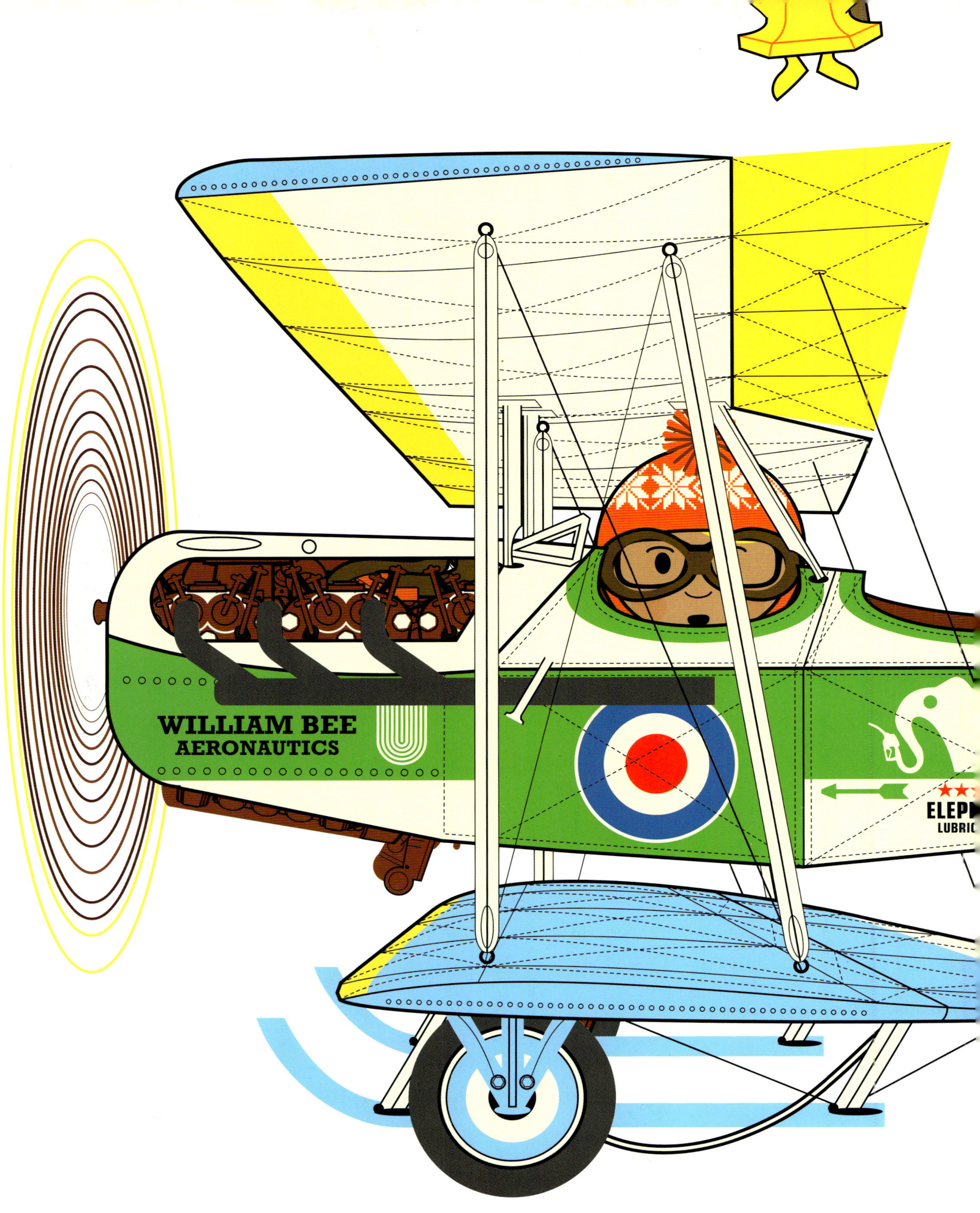
WILLIAM BEE
AERONAUTICS
ELEP
LUBRIC

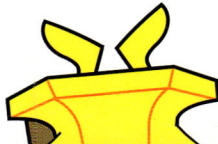

You need a *much* stronger plane to carry tonnes of water, like this fire-putting-out sea plane.

It dives down into the sea, scoops up lots and lots of sea water, and drops it on to the fire.

It can go where fire engines can't – like into the jungle, or up to the tops of mountains.

But luckily there aren't any fires today, so the best thing we can do in the sea is...

...skim across the tops of the waves in a super-fast super-streamlined supercharged speed boat!

If you want to go *under* the sea (and why wouldn't you?) then you need a submarine.

It's very useful if you want to find your super-fast, super-streamlined, supercharged speed boat – after it sinks.

ILLIAM BEE
NDERWATER
XPLORATION

There it is!

Can there be anywhere more extraordinary to go than down, down, down under the sea? Yes! You can go up, up, up into space!

But first you have to fill the rocket up, up, up with fuel. Twenty-three tankers worth of fuel.

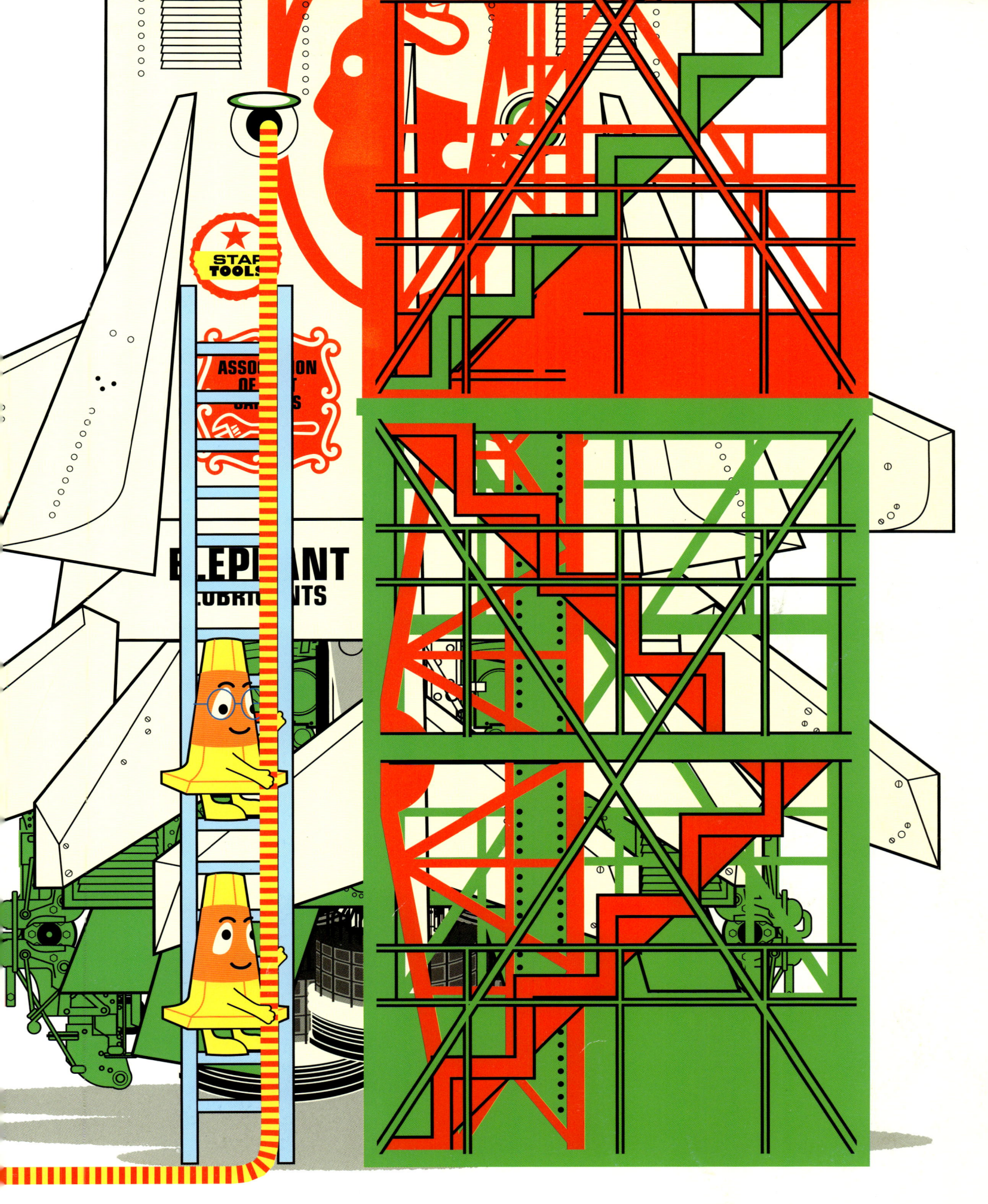

And then you have to go
up, up, up the steps.

Lots of them! Which is
hard work when you are
wearing space suits
and space boots.

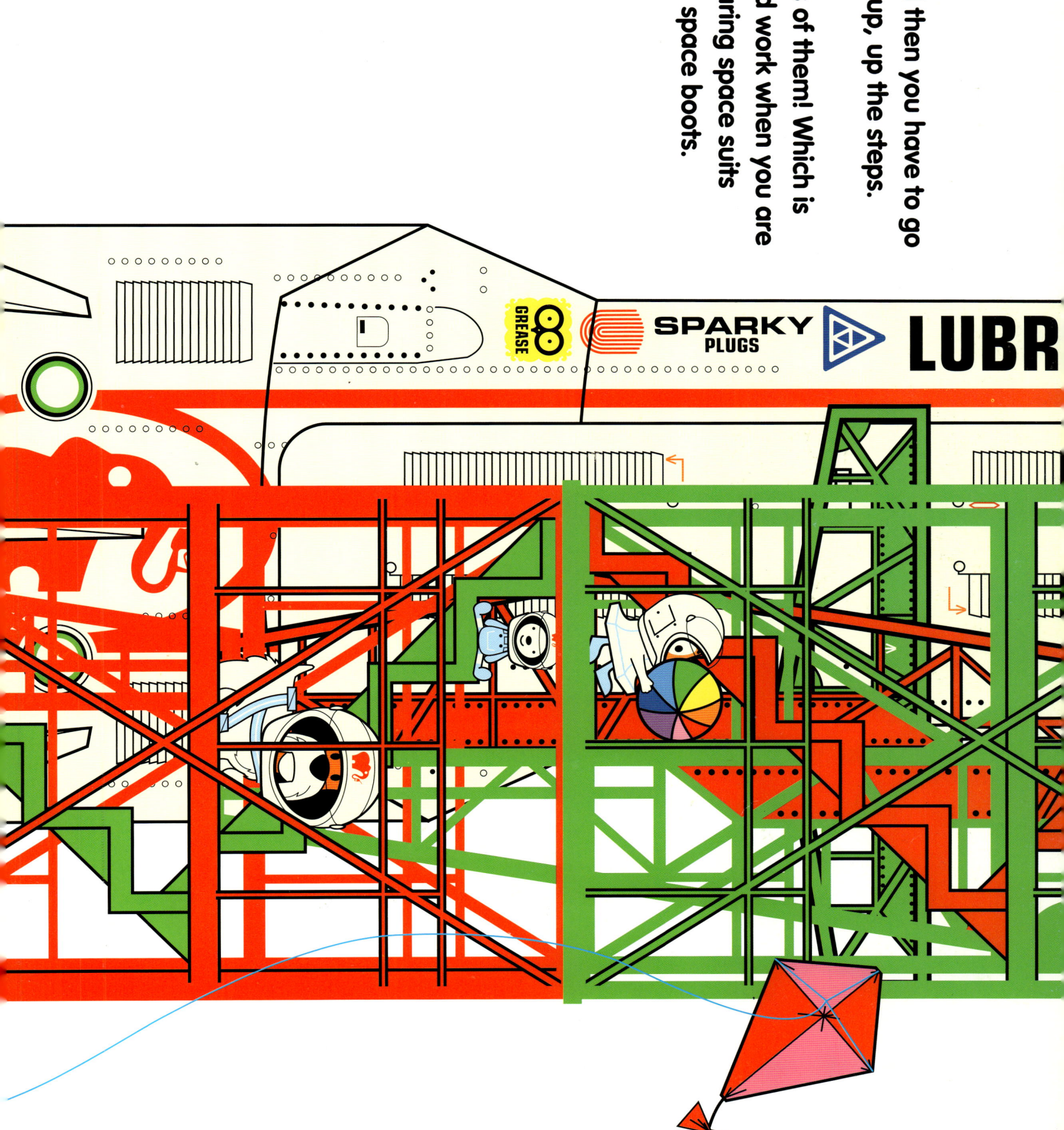

At last, we're at the top and ready to go!

10... 9... 8...

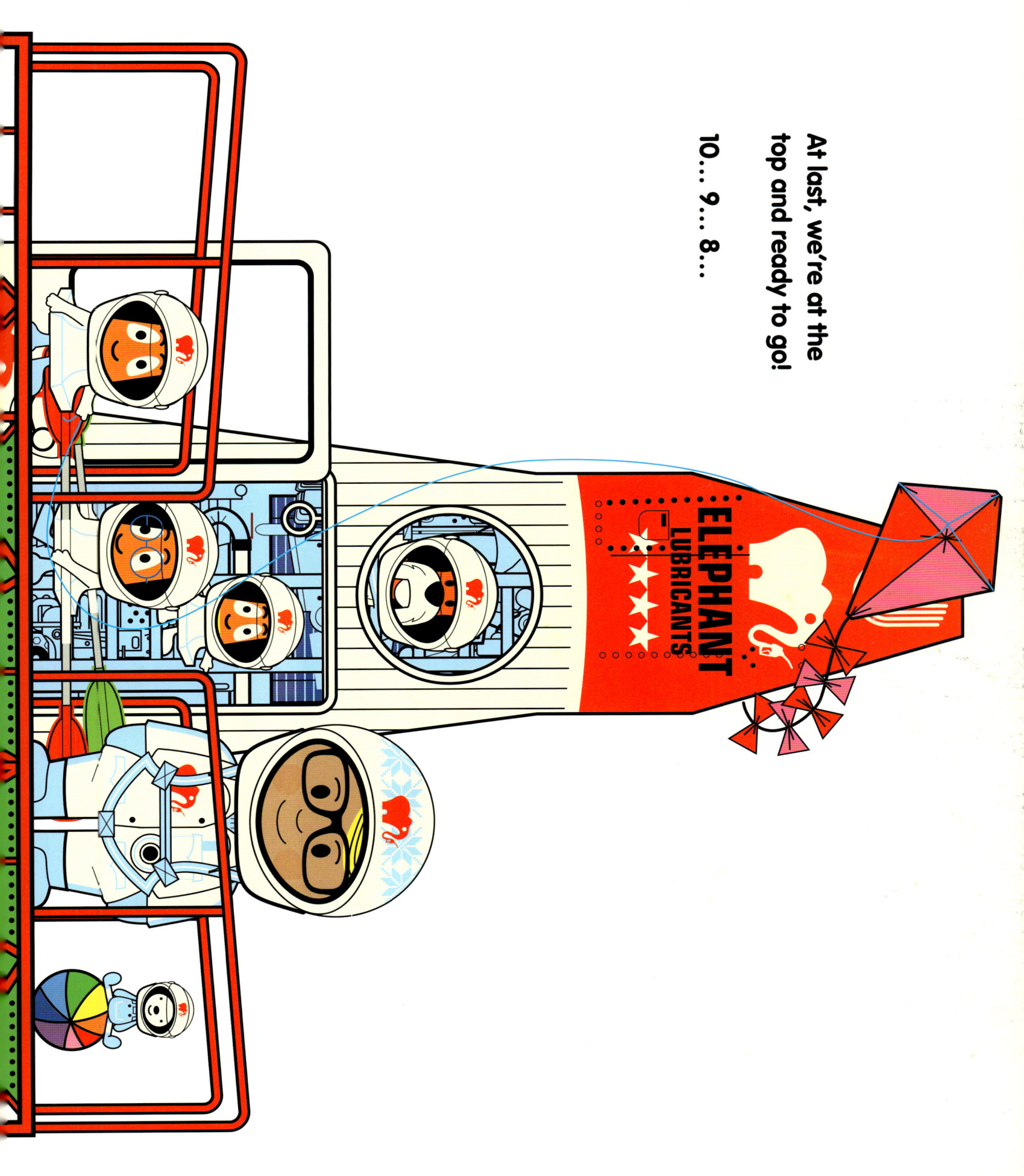

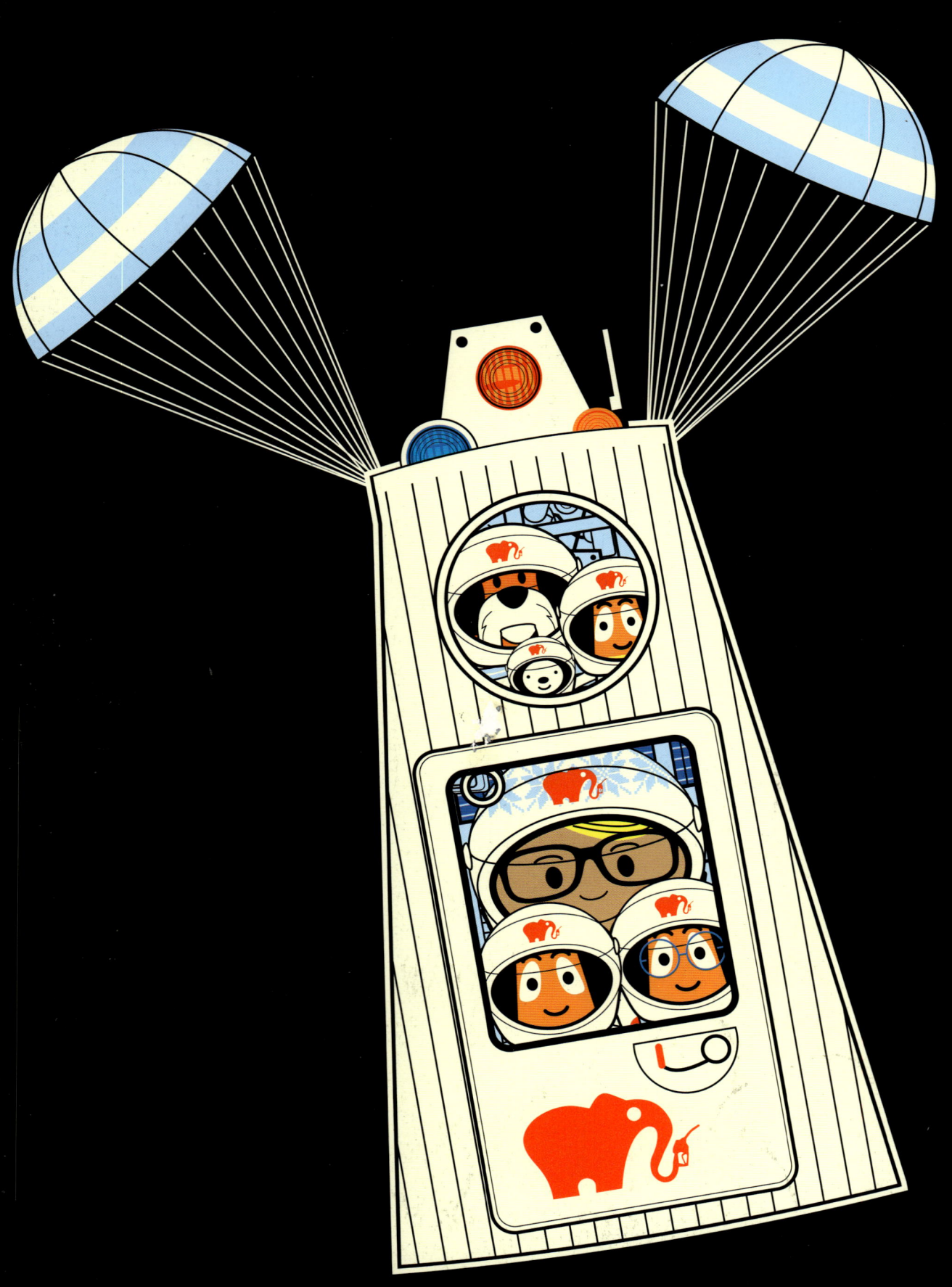

Well that was nice, the moon.

But it's time to get back to laying all that railway track, and maybe putting out a few mountain fires, and not forgetting that we need to get all the sea water out of my super-fast, super-streamlined, supercharged, super-soggy speed boat...

Now where ON EARTH are we going to land?

More coal-fired, space-exploring, jet-powered, hovercrafting facts from William Bee

Steam engines can be used to power trains, or trucks, or ships, or even machines that stand still and make things in factories.

They run on coal and water. The coal is used to make a fire, which heats the water up, and this creates steam which is piped into a cylinder and powers a piston, which goes backwards and forwards and makes the wheels turn.

Some of the steam 'escapes' from the train's funnel.

coal

water

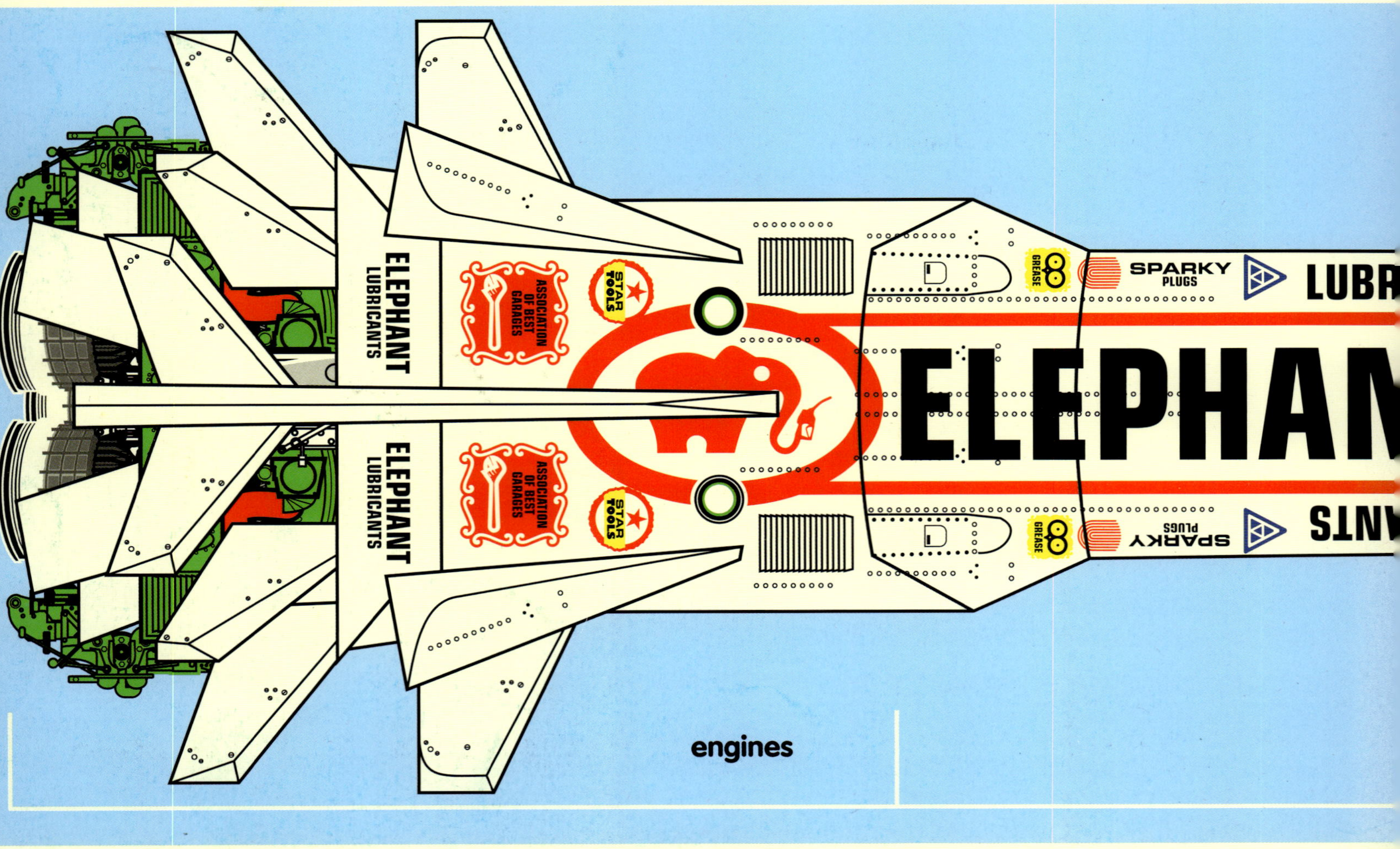

ELEPHANT LUBRICANTS

ELEPHANT LUBRICANTS

ASSOCIATION OF BEST GARAGES

ASSOCIATION OF BEST GARAGES

STAR TOOLS

STAR TOOLS

GREASE

GREASE

SPARKY PLUGS

SPARKY PLUGS

LUBR

ELEPHAN

ANTS

engines

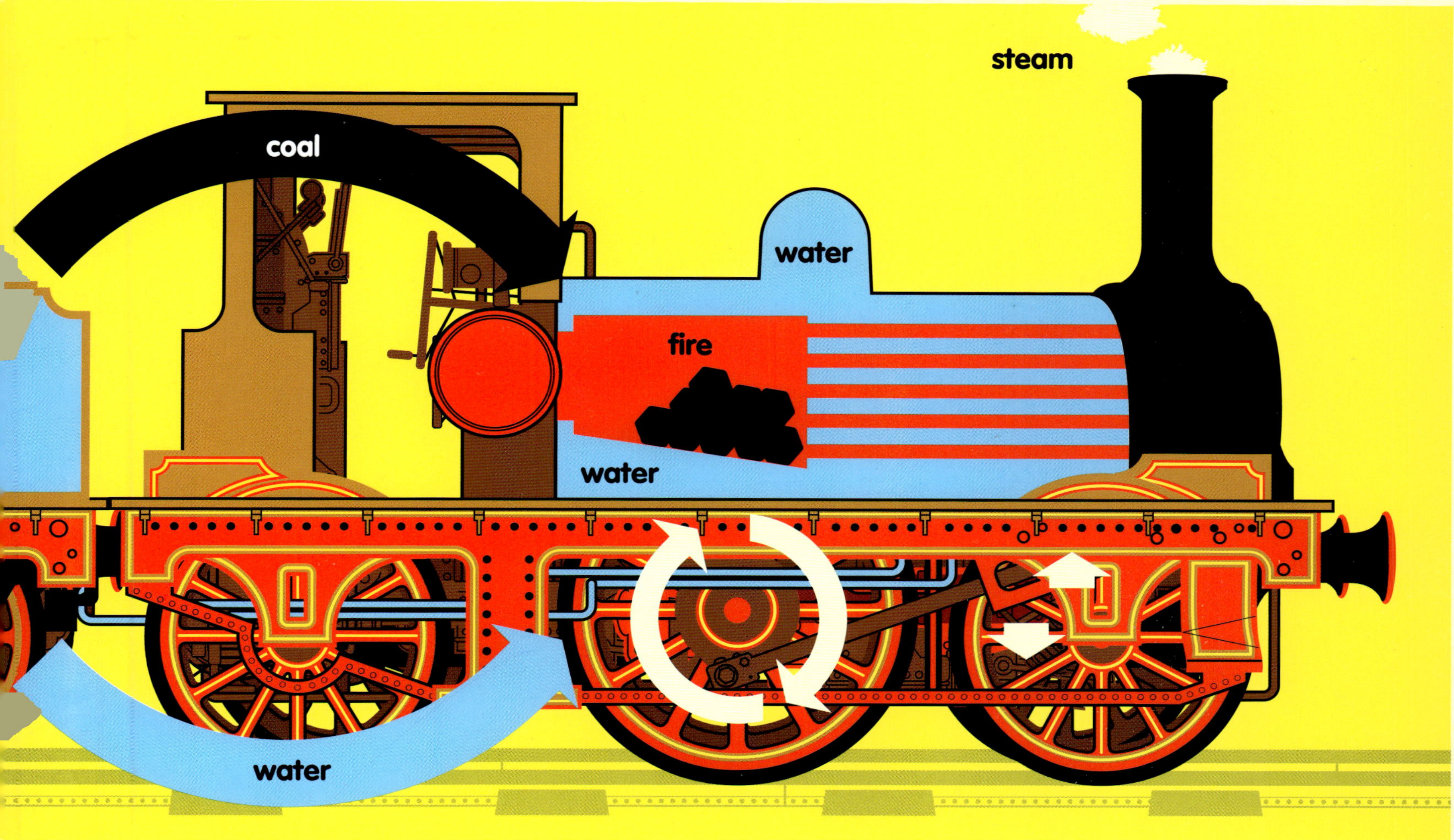

steam

coal

water

fire

water

water

William Bee's moon rocket is mostly made up of giant engines – three of them – and one great big fuel tank. It holds enough fuel to fill up 15,000 cars, and most of this gets used up in just a few minutes on take off to escape the Earth's gravity.

LUBRICANTS
LUBRICANTS

ELEPHANT
LUBRICANTS

fuel tank

astronauts' capsule

parachutes

This is how William Bee's vertical jump jet goes straight up – instead of needing a long runway like most aeroplanes. It has four 'nozzles' (two on each side – coloured yellow here), which turn so all the power from the engine is aimed downwards for take off.

William Bee's jump jet uses its engine to push it up into the air, and so does his hovercraft.

Two engines at the back power the big fans underneath (in green here), which push the air down, like the jump jet. But the 'skirts' (in pink here) stop most of the air from escaping and allow the hovercraft to float on a cushion of air. It can float over ground or water. The engine then moves it forward.

Then they turn to face backwards and push the plane forwards. When the plane wants to land, the nozzles turn down again and the power is decreased.

ELEPHANT
LUBRICANTS

ADVERTISEMENT

ELEPHANT WORKWEAR code M41
MECHANIC OVERALLS

ELEPHANT WORKWEAR code M42a
STEAM TRAIN DRIVER OVERALLS

ELEPHANT WORKWEAR code M41b
DIESEL TRAIN DRIVER OVERALLS

ELEPHANT WORKWEAR code B9xc
ELECTRIC TRAIN DRIVER
SHIRT, TIE AND TROUSERS

ELEPHANT WORKWEAR code D78a
HOVERCRAFT PILOT
WATERPROOFS

ELEPHANT WORKWEAR code LMx
JET FIGHTER PILOT FLIGHT SUIT

ELEPHANT WORKWEAR code LDcx
AVIATOR FLIGHT SUIT

ELEPHANT WORKWEAR code T16
FIRE SERVICE PILOT FLIGHT SUIT

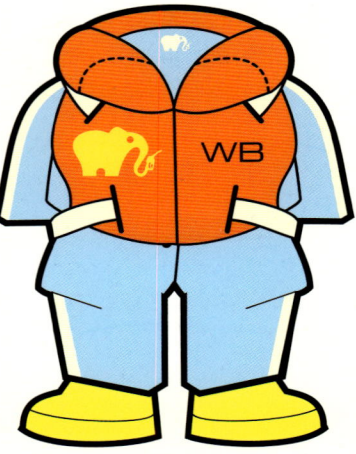

ELEPHANT WORKWEAR code D78b
SUBMARINER WATERPROOFS

Overalls available from **ELEPHANT** Service Stations and all good motor factors
All other **ELEPHANT WORKWEAR** available from all good workwear stockists

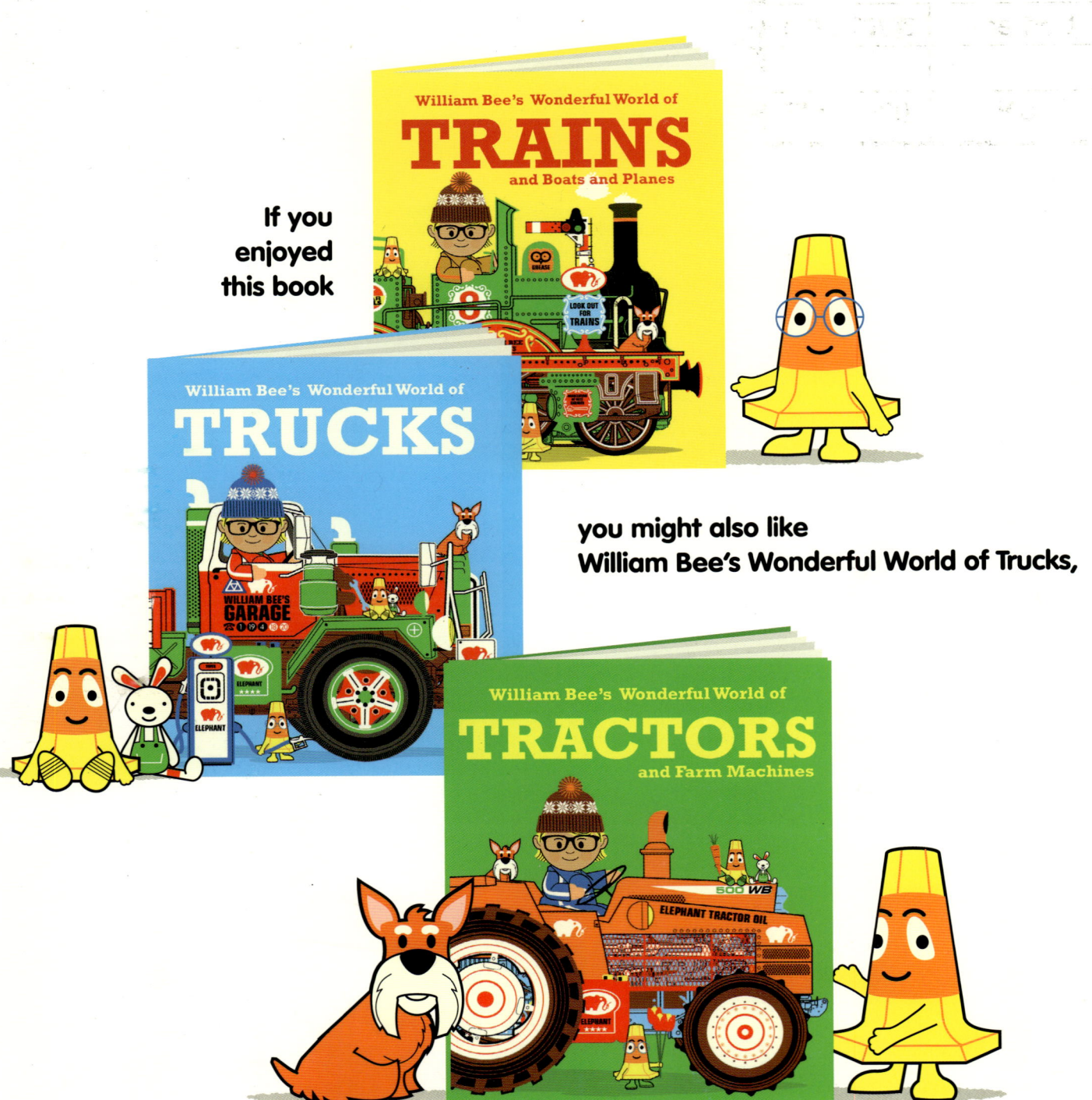

If you enjoyed this book

William Bee's Wonderful World of
TRAINS
and Boats and Planes

William Bee's Wonderful World of
TRUCKS

**you might also like
William Bee's Wonderful World of Trucks,**

William Bee's Wonderful World of
TRACTORS
and Farm Machines

**or William Bee's Wonderful World of
Tractors and Farm Machines**